Meet NASA Inventor Philip Lubin and His Team's

Laser-Sailing Starships

www.worldbook.com

World Book, Inc.
180 North LaSalle Street
Suite 900
Chicago, Illinois 60601
USA

For information about other World Book publications, visit our website at www.worldbook.com or call 1-800-WORLDBK (967-5325).

For information about sales to schools and libraries, call 1-800-975-3250 (United States), or 1-800-837-5365 (Canada).

Library of Congress Cataloging-in-Publication Data for this volume has been applied for.

Out of This World
978-0-7166-6155-9 (set, hc.)

Laser-Sailing Starships
ISBN: 978-0-7166-6159-7 (hc.)
ISBN: 978-0-7166-6135-1 (pf.)

Also available as:
ISBN: 978-0-7166-6168-9 (e-book)

Staff

Writer: Jeff De La Rosa

Executive Committee

President
Jim O'Rourke

Vice President and
Editor in Chief
Paul A. Kobasa

Vice President, Finance
Donald D. Keller

Vice President, Marketing
Jean Lin

Vice President, International Sales
Maksim Rutenberg

Director, Human Resources
Bev Ecker

Editorial

Director, Print Content
Development
Tom Evans

Editor, Print Content Development
Kendra Muntz

Managing Editor, Science
Jeff De La Rosa

Editor, Science
William D. Adams

Librarian
S. Thomas Richardson

Manager, Contracts & Compliance
(Rights & Permissions)
Loranne K. Shields

Manager, Indexing Services
David Pofelski

Administrative Assistant, Digital
and Print Content Development
Ethel Matthews

Digital

Director, Digital Content
Development
Emily Kline

Director, Digital Product
Development
Erika Meller

Manager, Digital Products
Jonathan Wills

Graphics and Design

Senior Art Director
Tom Evans

Senior Visual Communications
Designer
Melanie Bender

Media Researcher
Rosalia Bledsoe

Manufacturing/
Production

Manufacturing Manager
Anne Fritzinger

Proofreader
Nathalie Strassheim

Contents

Glossary There is a glossary of terms on page 45. Terms defined in the glossary are in boldface type that **looks like this** on their first appearance on any spread (two facing pages).

Pronunciations (how to say words) are given in parentheses the first time some difficult words appear in the book. They look like this: pronunciation (pruh NUHN see AY shuhn).

Introduction

Have you ever looked up at the night sky and dreamed of visiting a distant star? Just how long would it take to get there? Consider Arcturus (ahrkTUR uhs), for example, the brightest star in the northern sky. Arcturus is many times larger and about 100 times as *luminous* (bright) as our own star, the sun. But Arcturus is so far away that it appears as a tiny dot of light.

Arcturus is the bright star circled at right. Because it is so far away from Earth, we see it as a tiny point of light, even though it is much larger and brighter than the sun.

When seen in the sky, Arcturus seems to follow the group of stars, or constellation, called Ursa Major, the Great Bear. The name *Arcturus* comes from the Greek words meaning *bear watcher*.

Light travels faster than anything else, seeming to cross great distances in an instant. Light travels through empty space at about 186,282 miles (299,792 kilometers) per second. We call that the **speed of light.** Yet Arcturus is so far away that it takes its light about 37 years to reach Earth! The fastest spacecraft ever built, on the other hand, travel at only a tiny fraction of the speed of light. Chugging along at such slow speeds, it would take thousands of years to reach even the nearest star to the sun, Proxima Centauri.

The enormous **interstellar** distances would seem to put the stars beyond human reach. But the physicist Philip Lubin thinks he knows how to speed the journey. (A physicist is a scientist who studies matter—the stuff everything is made of—and energy.) There are two factors that help limit the speed to which we can **accelerate** a spacecraft. The first is the **mass** of the spacecraft. The second is the speed at which it can be pushed.

Traditional space **probes** are around the size of an automobile. The probes Lubin wants to create are much smaller—small enough to fit in your pocket. But the real trick comes in how you push them. Ordinary rockets are much too slow to cross the vast distances between Earth and the stars. To reach the necessary speeds, our pocket-sized probes will have to harness light itself, using special sails to hitch a ride on a **laser** beam.

Lubin estimates that such laser-sailing star voyagers could be accelerated to around one-third the speed of light. If so, they might be able to reach Proxima Centauri in under 20 years, becoming the first visitors to a neighboring **star system.**

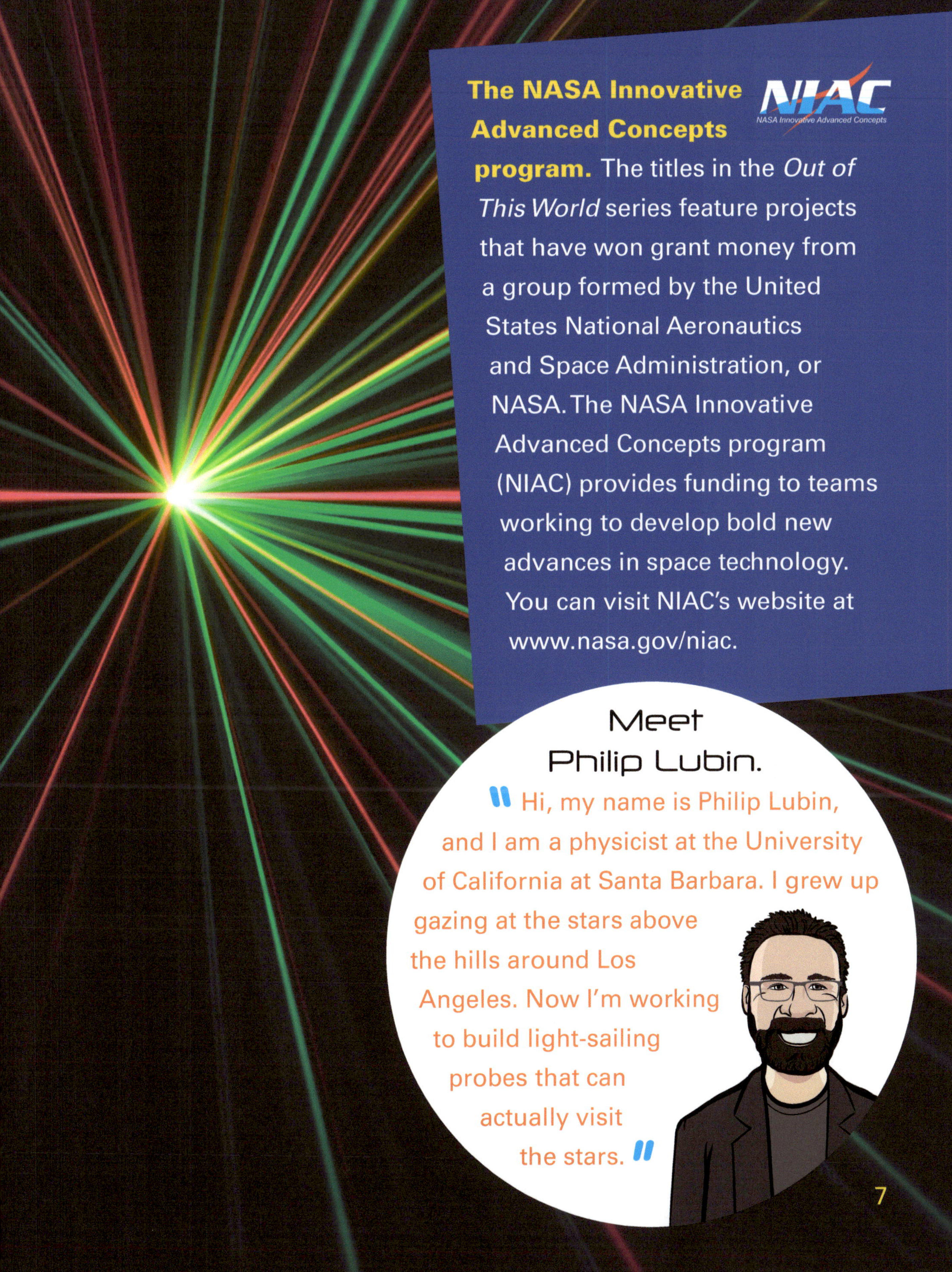

The NASA Innovative Advanced Concepts program. The titles in the *Out of This World* series feature projects that have won grant money from a group formed by the United States National Aeronautics and Space Administration, or NASA. The NASA Innovative Advanced Concepts program (NIAC) provides funding to teams working to develop bold new advances in space technology. You can visit NIAC's website at www.nasa.gov/niac.

Meet Philip Lubin.

"Hi, my name is Philip Lubin, and I am a physicist at the University of California at Santa Barbara. I grew up gazing at the stars above the hills around Los Angeles. Now I'm working to build light-sailing probes that can actually visit the stars."

Destination: Proxima Centauri

Proxima Centauri is the nearest star to our sun. It lies a little over 4 **light-years** away in the constellation Centaurus, the Centaur. (The name *Proxima Centauri* means *the nearest star in Centaurus.* And a *centaur* is an imaginary animal, half man and half horse.) A light-year is the distance light travels in one year, about 5.88 trillion miles (9.46 trillion kilometers).

In 2016, astronomers studying light from Proxima Centauri discovered evidence that the star has a planet, called Proxima Centauri b. Scientists believe that Proxima Centauri b is a rocky planet just a little bit larger than Earth. It appears to orbit, or travel around, its star about once every 11 Earth days.

Scientists are particularly excited that the planet appears to orbit within Proxima Centauri's habitable zone. The habitable zone is the region around a star in which liquid water can exist on a planet's surface. This discovery raises the possibility that the planet could be home to life. The surface of Proxima Centauri b probably receives much more radiation from its star than Earth receives from the sun, suggesting harsh conditions. But scientists know little about the

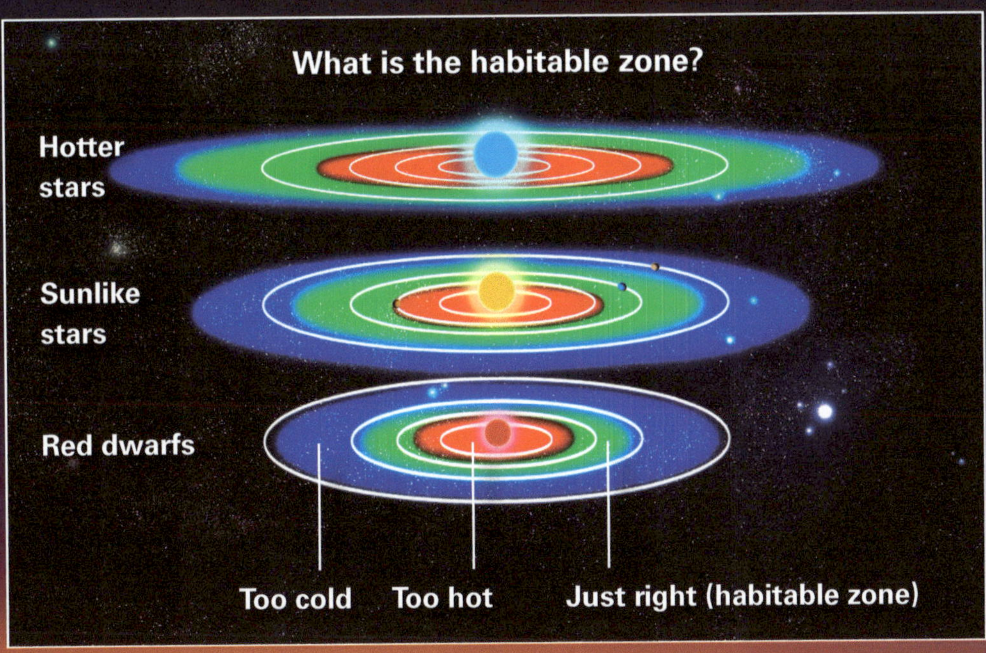

kinds of life that may exist in other **star systems,** making the Proxima Centauri system a tempting target for exploration.

Red dwarf. Proxima Centauri is a kind of star called a red dwarf. Red dwarfs are the most common type of star in our galaxy. They are smaller and fainter than our sun. Proxima Centauri is about one-eighth the sun's size. It is too faint to be seen without a telescope. The Scottish astronomer Robert Innes discovered Proxima Centauri in 1915.

Artist's depiction of Proxima Centauri b's rocky surface.

How many worlds? Astronomers once thought that stars with planets might be rare, making our own solar system pretty special.

"However, we know from recent studies, such as the Kepler project, that there is about one planet per star on average. That is a revolution in our understanding. We did not realize how common planets were." —Philip

Kepler is a space telescope that in 2009 began surveying distant stars. It looked for tiny changes in the brightness of each star that would suggest a planet had passed in front of it. Kepler identified thousands of exoplanets (planets orbiting distant stars), with some stars having no planets and a small number having several.

Follow the water

On Earth, life is found just about everywhere we look. Hardy living things survive in the bitter chill of Antarctica, the heat of underwater volcanic vents, and the heights of Earth's atmosphere. But everywhere life is found it requires some kind of water. So, in searching for life in other parts of the universe, scientists look for places where liquid water may be found. If a planet is too close to its parent star, any water would boil away. If the planet is too far, its water would remain frozen as ice. The region between these two extremes is called the habitable zone.

The space telescope Kepler, shown here in this artist's impression, has identified thousands of exoplanets. The telescope is named for Johannes Kepler, a German astronomer and mathematician who lived from 1571 to 1630.

Inventor feature:

Growing up during the space race

"I grew up in the 1950's and 1960's, when the space race was very much on the minds of people around the world." —Philip

The space race was a period of intense competition in space exploration between the United States and the Soviet Union (a country that existed from 1922 to1991). This competition pushed scientists in both countries to achieve many new milestones in space exploration. The Soviet Union earned many early victories. On Oct. 4, 1957, the Soviets launched the first artificial satellite, Sputnik 1, into orbit. The Soviet Union also launched the first person into space, cosmonaut Yuri Gagarin, on April 12, 1961.

"I remember as a child building little spacecraft and being fascinated by the whole idea. I built a rocket out of cardboard. Then I crawled inside and pretended I was an astronaut." —Philip

The United States entered the era of piloted space exploration with the Mercury and Gemini programs. The Apollo program landed people on the moon on July 20, 1969, the last major milestone of the space race.

"I thought it was incredible for humans to walk on the moon. I was in high school at the time, and I was just transfixed by that whole moment." —Philip

The space race captured the imagination of Lubin and many other young people at the time, inspiring them to become the next generation of cosmic explorers.

Astronaut Buzz Aldrin salutes the U.S. flag on the surface of the moon.

Interstellar travel

Proxima Centauri may be the sun's next-door neighbor by cosmic standards, but four **light-years** is still an incredible distance to travel. What is the fastest thing you can think of? A racecar? A jet airplane?

A typical jet airliner travels about 500 miles (800 kilometers) per hour. That is fast enough to fly halfway around the world in a day. But at that speed, it would still take tens of thousands of years to reach Proxima Centauri, much longer than the time since people several thousand years ago started keeping track of things!

Spacecraft can actually travel much faster than a jet airliner. In 2006, NASA launched the New Horizons **probe** to the dwarf planet Pluto. The craft left Earth orbit at record speed, moving about 80 times as fast as our jet. Even moving at such great speed, it took New Horizons nine years to reach Pluto. And Pluto is not even near the edge of our solar system. At similar speeds, it would take a probe hundreds of years to reach Proxima Centauri.

The spacecraft that has made it farthest from Earth is Voyager 1. This probe was launched in 1977 to explore the outer planets of our solar system. It swung by Jupiter in 1979 and Saturn in 1980, before flinging itself off toward **interstellar** space. Traveling at a speed similar to that of New Horizons, the craft took more than 35 years to reach the edge of the solar system.

Voyager 1, launched in 1977, took more than 35 years to reach the edge of the solar system.

NASA's New Horizons probe, lauched with a conventional rocket as shown here, took nine years to reach the dwarf planet Pluto.

Getting there faster

Such long travel times do not just make scientists impatient. In fact, they seem to place the stars beyond our reach. But Phil Lubin has come up with an idea for reaching Proxima Centauri within 20 to 30 years. His plan is ambitious. Surprisingly, it does not require some outstanding breakthrough in science. Rather, it can be built using and developing existing technologies.

"We would like to be able to go faster and farther in space exploration than is currently possible. To do that, we have to change the way in which we propel spacecraft. And to some extent, we have to change our idea of what a spacecraft is." —Philip

In this illustration, a simple sail craft—the curved gray object at the right— is propelled from Earth by powerful lasers.

To understand Lubin's plan, we must first think about what it takes to **accelerate** something. To do so, we must apply a force on the object.

Imagine pushing a wagon as hard as you can. If the wagon was empty, your push might quickly get the wagon moving. But if the wagon was full of heavy rocks, the same push might not get the wagon moving at all! The wagon's acceleration depends in part on its **mass.**

The relationship between the force (F) of a push, the object's mass (m), and its acceleration (a) is shown in this mathematical formula:

$$F = ma$$

That is, the force equals the mass times the acceleration. The equation can also be rearranged in the following way:

$$a = F/m$$

This means that for a particular force, as the mass of the object increases, the acceleration decreases. On the other hand, as the mass of the object decreases, the acceleration increases.

The bottom line is that the smaller something is, the easier it is to accelerate it to extremely high speeds. So the first part of Lubin's plan involves making a space **probe** as small as possible.

The acceleration of this wheelbarrow depends on the strength of the man pushing it and the weight of the child riding in it.

Big idea:
Make it smaller

In some ways, the history of engineering can be seen as a quest to make things bigger. Advances in engineering have given us larger ships, taller skyscrapers, and longer bridges. Sending astronauts to the moon was the greatest feat yet in human space exploration, and it required the largest rocket ever built: the 363-foot- (111-meter-) tall Saturn V.

In electronics, though, making things smaller has been the main goal. The first electronic computers, built in the 1940's, were as big as a room. They made calculations using thousands of bulky devices called vacuum tubes. In the 1950's, the vacuum tubes were replaced with smaller devices called transistors.

The trend of making electronics smaller continued in the 1960's with the development of the integrated circuit, sometimes called the computer chip. An integrated circuit is basically lots of tiny switches etched into a chip of **semiconductor** material, usually **silicon.** Through

ENIAC was one of the first useful computers. It filled an entire room and required a team of workers to operate it.

advances in materials and manufacturing, the number of devices that can be etched onto a chip has increased faster and faster. Since the mid-1970's, that number has doubled about every two years. As a result, computers have become much more powerful, even as they have become smaller.

Big idea:
Make it smaller
cont.

"You can see this in your own life by looking at tablet computers and smartphones. Every year, new ones come out that are smaller or thinner and more powerful." —Philip

As computer chips have shrunk, so have other electronic components, such as **sensors** and cameras. A robotic space **probe** is in some ways a collection of electronic devices sent into space. Traditional space probes weigh many hundreds or thousands of pounds or kilograms on Earth. But by using the smallest possible devices, Lubin envisions a much smaller probe.

"It's possible to imagine putting an entire spacecraft onto something the same size as a smart phone. A smartphone has a camera. It has a system for sending and receiving data. It has sensors that can detect motion and changes in position. That got me thinking—why don't we fly cell phones instead of traditional space probes?" —Philip

The first mobile phones (left) were simple and bulky. Modern smartphones, such as the one above, use much-improved cell phone technology while fitting in the palm of a hand. They also have computing power many thousands of times greater than that of the room-sized ENIAC.

Moore's law. The idea that the number of devices that can be placed on a computer chip doubles about every two years is called Moore's law. It is named for the American research scientist Gordon Moore (1929-), who noted that the number was doubling on a regular basis. Moore's law has pushed computer scientists and computer makers to build smaller and more powerful computers.

Inventor feature:

Phil Fix-it

Lubin started his career not as an inventor, but as a theoretical physicist. Theoretical physics involves the use of mathematics and reasoning to develop our understanding of matter, energy, and the universe.

"I was very oriented toward *pure mathematics* [the study of mathematics for its own sake] and fundamental physics. I shifted a bit when I started studying the structure of the early universe." —Philip

To study the early universe, scientists begin by making measurements of the universe today. To accomplish his work, Lubin had to help develop detectors and other equipment to make the measurements he needed.

"In order to explore, one often has to build things." —Philip

Getting involved in technology gave Lubin a chance to return to his childhood interests. As a youth, he was fascinated with how things work. He indulged his curiosity by taking things apart and putting them back together.

" I was very comfortable as a child building things and tearing them apart. I liked to use my hands. " —Philip

Lubin took apart radios and television sets. He worked on engines and was fascinated by electronics. His constant tinkering earned him the nickname Phil Fix-it.

Philip with his dad in 1955, *left,* and as a student at Harvard, *above.*

Pushing faster

" To some extent, making smaller spacecraft is the easier piece of the puzzle. There's already an entire industry working to develop smaller, more powerful, more cost-efficient electronics. " —Philip

Mass is only part of the equation, though. In conventional spacecraft, propulsion—the push—is generally provided by rockets. But rockets are heavy and require heavy *propellants* (fuels). Attaching a rocket would add too much mass to Lubin's tiny **probes.** To **accelerate** spacecraft to speeds that have never been reached, Lubin also needs a new way to push them.

Luckily, there is another way to push something. Imagine a boat sailing on the water. The force that moves the boat does not come from the boat itself. Instead, it comes from the push of the wind against the boat's sails.

To push Lubin's tiny probe, he might attach a sail to it. But there is no wind in space to push against the sail. Even if there was, everyday winds could not push the probe fast enough. To push Lubin's probes, he needs to find something faster.

" And the fastest thing that we have is light. " —Philip

People have been using sails to move boats and ships for thousands of years. These sails catch gusts of wind to push the vessel. Other types of sails can be used in space.

Big idea: Solar sails

As strange as it may sound, scientists have already begun experimenting with spacecraft that sail on light. Such designs are often called solar sails, because they use the pressure of sunlight to move through space.

A solar sail consists of a lightweight framework covered in a large sheet of reflective material. The "wind" in space takes the form of **photons** given off by the sun.

When a photon bumps into a solar sail, the mirrored surface reflects the photon back into space. At the same time, some of the photon's **momentum** is transferred to the sail. Solar sails are using the third law of motion developed by the English scientist Isaac Newton (1642-1727). That law says that for each action there is an equal and opposite reaction. So, the reflection of the photon pushes the sail in the opposite direction.

Photons do not have much momentum, so not much push is transferred to the sail. But over time, as millions and millions of photons strike it, the force multiplies and the sail can be **accelerated** to speeds close to the **speed of light.**

Designing a solar sail. Because the momentum carried by an individual photon is extremely small, solar sails must be large enough to catch millions of photons. Some sail designs could have as much area as 1 to 10 football fields. To obtain as much speed as possible, solar sails also must be lightweight. Some experimental sails have been made of material that is about one-third the thickness of typical plastic wrap. Solar sails must also be near-perfect reflectors. The more reflective the sails are, the more the momentum of photons is converted into motion—and the faster the sail goes.

Solar sails use photons to accelerate a spacecraft.

Inventor feature:

Observing nature

Lubin's interest in exploration comes in part from his fascination with nature and the outdoors.

" I used to surf a lot when I was younger. As a child, it used to be a great thing to just get together and go to the beach and hang out, take our surf boards to the beach and go surfing. " —Philip

Lubin was fascinated by the stars. But he grew up in Los Angeles, and bright, hazy city skies don't make for good stargazing.

" When I got a little bit older, I liked to go hiking up in the mountains. It was like removing a fog from the sky. Suddenly, I could see that this beautiful universe existed. I think it sparked a lot of my imagination to want to explore more. " —Philip

Lubin still enjoys hiking. He loves to go out in the snow and enjoy the deep winter.

" I look up in the sky and imagine what's up there. "

—Philip

Philip poses in front of the slopes with his snowboard.

Laser power

A solar sail-powered craft could be suited to travel the vast distances between Earth and nearby stars. But there are two major problems. First, the craft would take a long time to reach **interstellar** speeds. Second, as the craft got farther and farther from the sun, there would be fewer and fewer **photons** to keep driving the sail forward.

" To continue the idea of sailing, you have this sailboat, but the wind is not strong enough to make it go. You need some way to blow on it. " —Philip

To drive a light sail quickly to interstellar speeds, Lubin would "blow" on it by using a form of light much more intense than sunlight: the **laser.**

Light can be thought of as a particle—the photon—but it also behaves in some ways like a wave you might see in the water. In sunlight, and many other kinds of natural light, the waves go all over the place. They move in different directions; they have different lengths from the top, or peak, of one wave to the peak of the next; and the "valleys," or troughs, between the tops usually don't line up.

In laser light, on the other hand, all the waves move the same way. The waves have the same length, and they line up peak to peak and trough to trough. As a result, laser light can travel as a very narrow beam over long distances. Other kinds of light spread out quickly and fade after a short distance.

In this photograph, an observatory shines a laser at a spacecraft orbiting the moon. Since all the light waves from a laser move in the same direction (inset), the beam can travel long distances without fading.

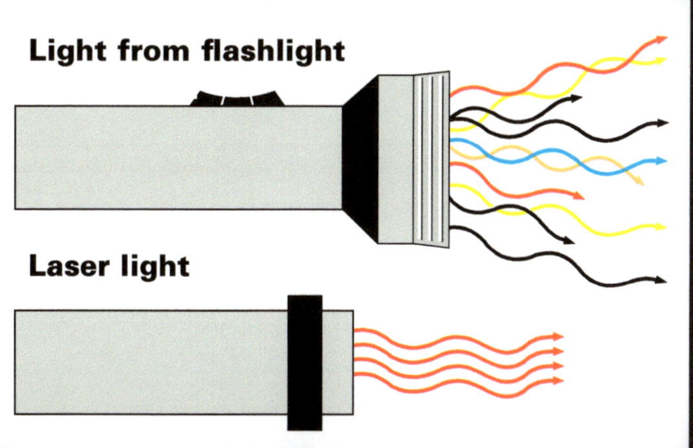

To understand Lubin's idea think of the traditional solar sail, slowly gaining **momentum,** as photons of sunlight from here and there blunder into it. Now imagine those photons are photons of laser light—large numbers of them zipping along in lockstep. Such a beam could give a lot of momentum to a light sail very quickly.

To provide even more power, several lasers could be made to go off together, their light combining to form one giant beam. This arrangement is called a **phased laser array.**

Unlike a traditional rocket engine, the phased laser array can be easily reused. And, because Lubin's tiny spacecraft should be relatively cheap, mission controllers could send many of them hurtling toward the stars one after another.

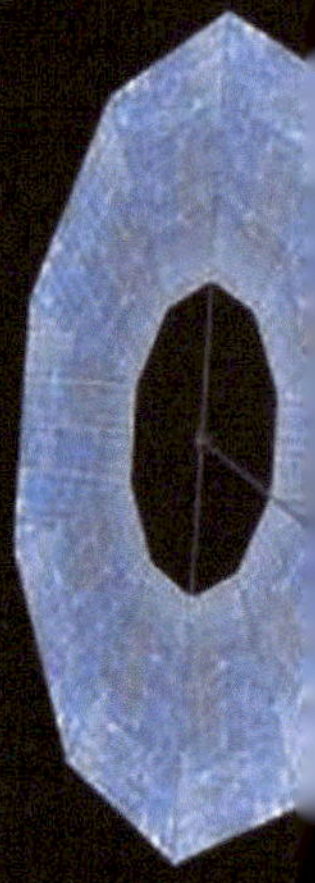

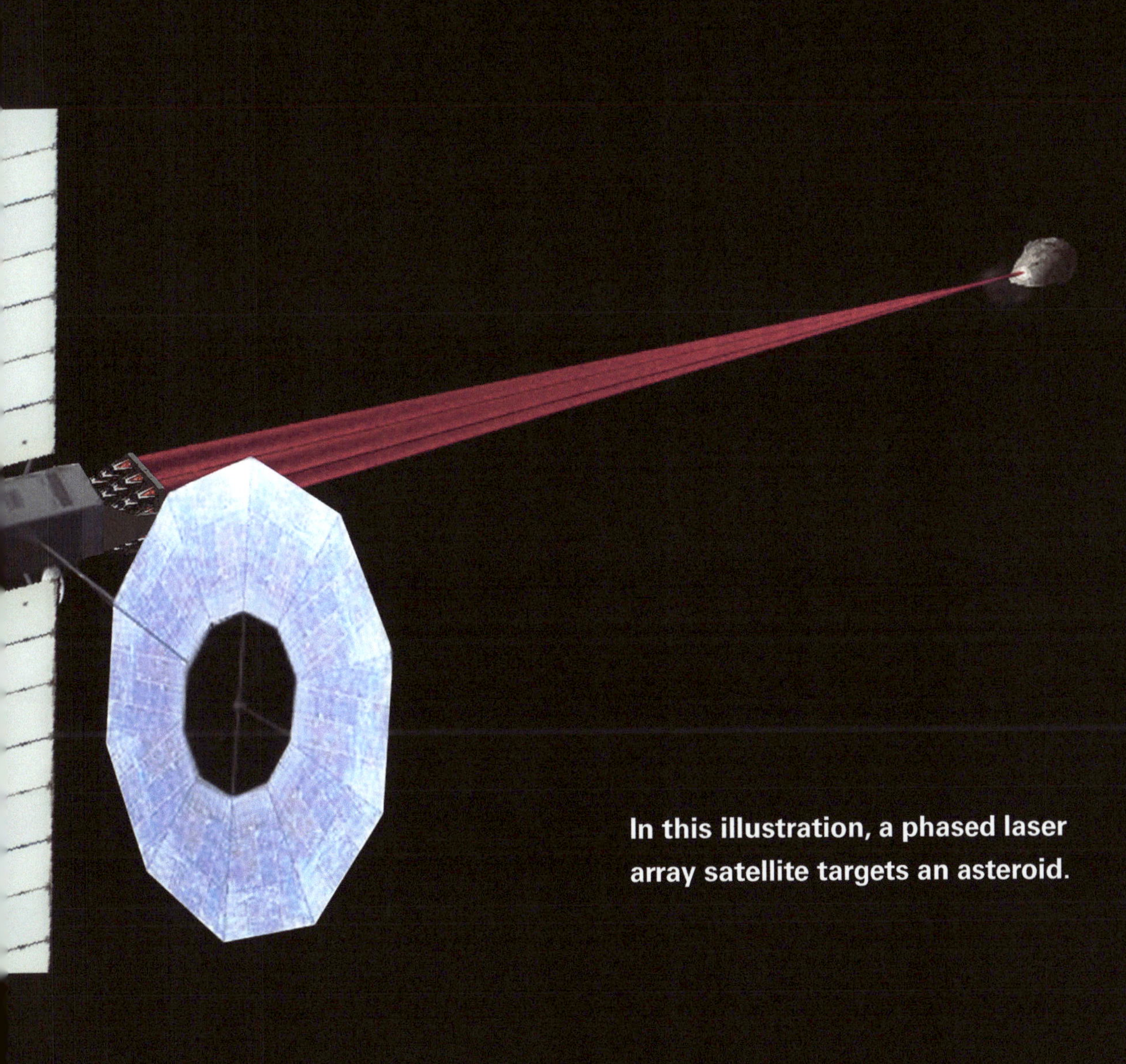

In this illustration, a phased laser array satellite targets an asteroid.

Inventor feature:

Defending the planet

Lubin actually began experimenting with **phased laser arrays** as a solution to a very different problem.

"We started looking at lasers for planetary defense, for deflecting asteroids." —Philip

Our solar system is littered with millions of rocky and metallic asteroids. Occasionally, one of these objects strikes Earth. Most of them burn up in the atmosphere, but larger asteroids can strike the ground, kicking up huge amounts of dust and triggering environmental disasters. Most scientists think that the damage caused by one such impact triggered the extinction of the dinosaurs and many other living things on Earth about 65 million years ago.

Such massive strikes are extremely rare. But scientists are thinking about ways to prevent them in the future.

"The same technology to protect the planet would also allow **interstellar** exploration. It is the same device, actually." —Philip

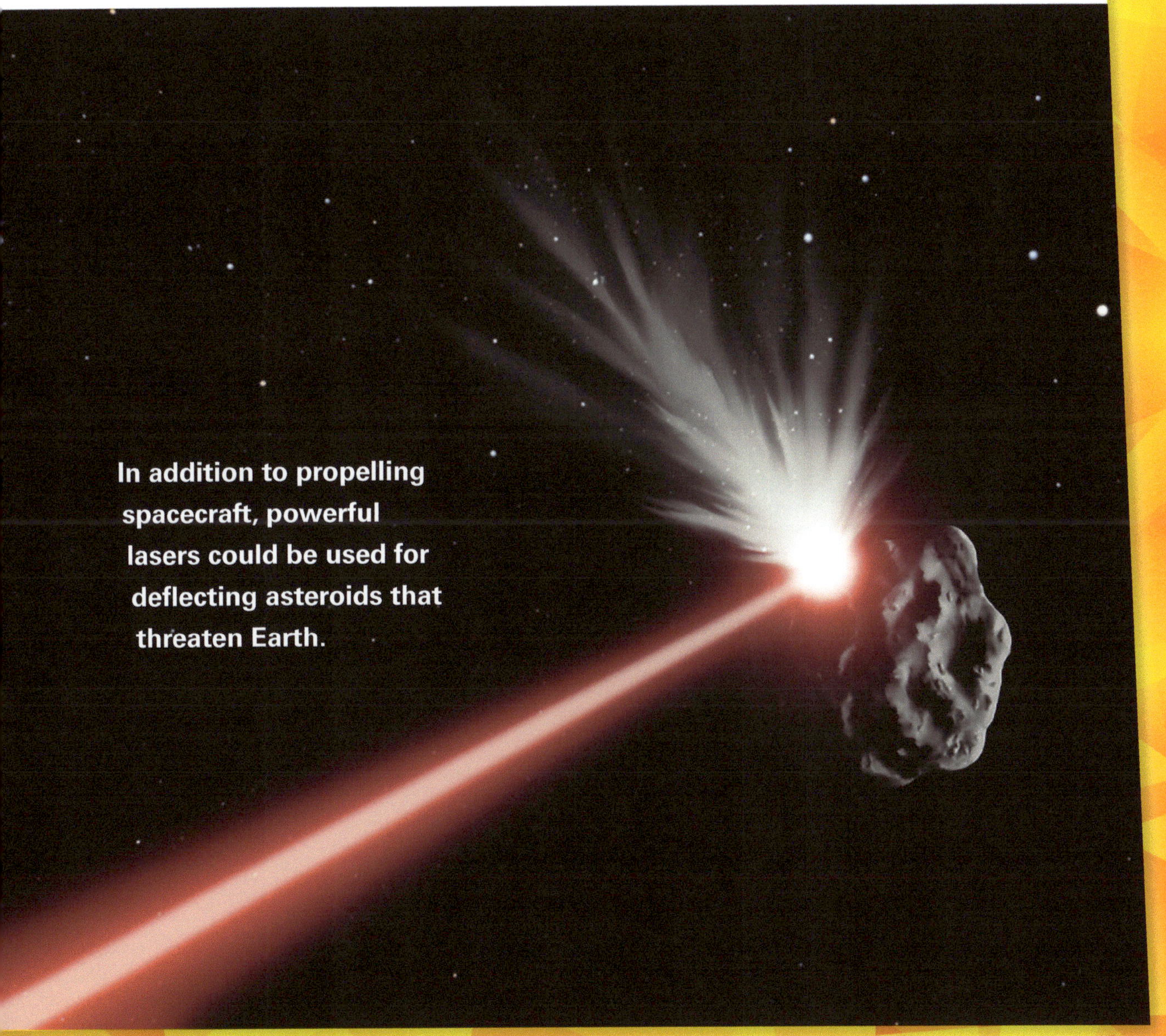

In addition to propelling spacecraft, powerful lasers could be used for deflecting asteroids that threaten Earth.

Proxima b or bust

So what might a future mission to Proxima b be like? Picture a launching station in orbit around Earth or perhaps on the surface of the moon. The station includes a **phased laser array.** One by one, the array targets a small fleet of light sails, each attached to a postage stamp-sized spacecraft.

It only takes a few minutes of **laser** illumination to propel each craft to about one-third the **speed of light.** In the first day, each craft will make it farther than Voyager 2 has traveled in over 35 years.

On Earth, flying objects slow down over time through **friction** with the air. In space, however, there is very little to slow our laser-sailing starships. Proxima Centauri is 4 **light-years** away. So even zipping along at one-third the speed of

Just 20 years after the launch of Lubin's tiny spacecraft, astronomers could be receiving close-up pictures of Proxima b.

light, it will take the tiny spacecraft 12 years to reach their destination.

As the spacecraft near Proxima Centauri and its planet, Proxima b, they will capture images and use **sensors** to gather other kinds of data. They will transmit this data back to Earth using lasers as well. Then, traveling much too fast to be stopped, they will continue to fly off into the emptiness of **interstellar** space.

Because Proxima Centauri is 4 light-years away, it will take 4 years for data sent by the spacecraft to be received back on Earth. Around 20 years after the launch, scientists could be looking at something once thought impossible: the first close-up pictures of a distant planetary system.

Ask Philip Lubin:

Can we visit the stars?

" The solar system is within our reach. Within our lifetimes, we will send people to Mars to explore the Martian surface. "

—Philip

Sending people to the stars is a much more difficult goal. Compared to Lubin's tiny spacecraft, human beings are heavy, and they need lots of heavy food, water, and air to keep them alive. It is difficult to imagine how to **accelerate** a human's **mass** to a reasonable speed for the **interstellar** trip.

" Eventually, I believe we will send visitors to other stars. But that is in the much more distant future. " —Philip

Inventor feature:

Childhood inspiration

Lubin remembers as a child being impressed with the movie *The Day the Earth Stood Still* (1951).

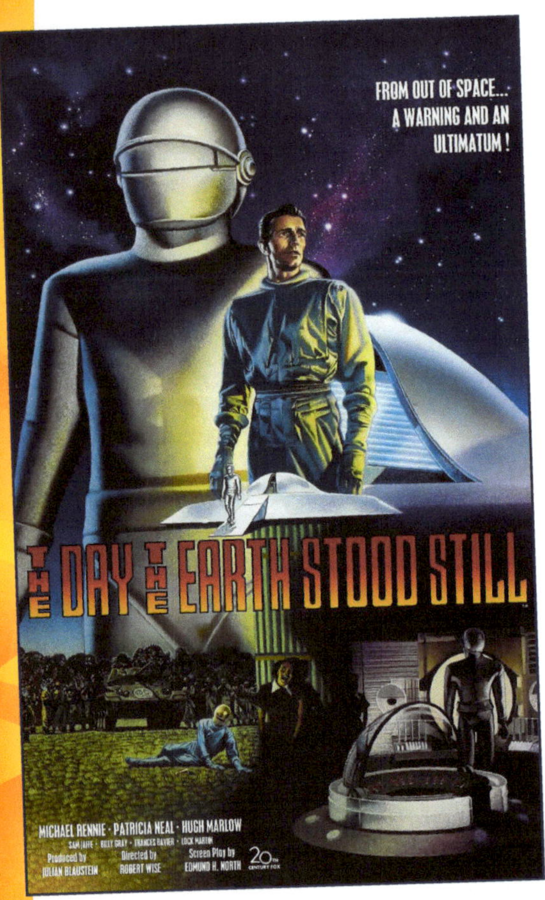

" It was an interesting commentary on both the possibilities of space exploration and societal issues related to exploration. " —Philip

In the film, an alien visitor arrives on Earth as human beings are beginning to explore space. He is greeted with suspicion and violence and eventually killed.

In the end, he delivers a serious message: Humans may continue to explore space, but if they bring violence with them, aliens will destroy Earth.

" That made a significant impression on me. I thought, why can't people just work together to do wonderful things instead of fighting one another? " —Philip

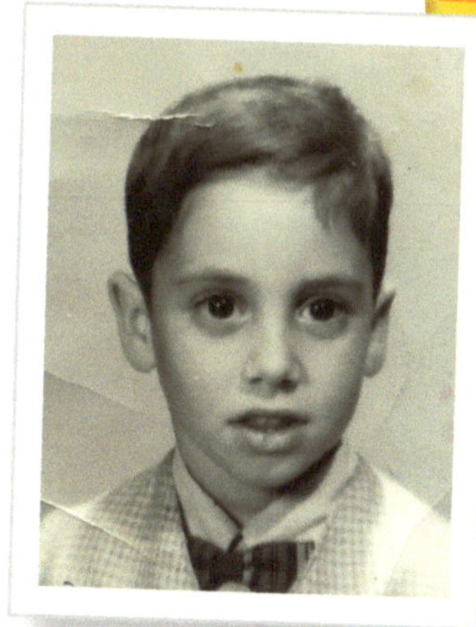

Philip as a grade school student in 1958.

As a child, Lubin would ride his bicycle to the library to read books on mathematics and science.

" I wanted to understand everything I could. "

—Philip

He also enjoyed the magazines *Popular Science* and *Popular Mechanics*.

Popular Science is an American magazine that features articles on science and technology written for a general audience. It was first published as *The Popular Science Monthly* in 1872.

Popular Mechanics is an American magazine that features articles on technology, including projects that can be tried in the home. It was first published in 1902.

Philip Lubin and his team

Professor Lubin and the Experimental Cosmology Group, part of the University of California, Santa Barbara Physics Department.

Glossary

accelerate (ak SEHL uh rayt) to change speed, to speed up.

friction (FRIHK shuhn) the resistance of a body in motion to the air, water, or other medium through which it travels or to the surface on which it travels.

interstellar (ihn tuhr STEHL uhr) between the stars.

laser (LAY zuhr) very powerful beam of light; also, the machine that makes such a beam.

light-year the distance light travels in a vacuum in one year, about 5.88 trillion miles (9.46 trillion kilometers).

mass the amount of matter in something.

momentum (moh MEHN tuhm) an object's amount of motion.

phased laser array (fayzd LAY zuhr ah RAY) multiple lasers connected to produce a single powerful beam.

photons (FOH tonz) tiny particles of light.

probe (prohb) a rocket, satellite, or other unmanned spacecraft carrying scientific instruments, to record or report back information about space.

semiconductor (SEHM ee kuhn DUHK tuhr) a material that conducts electric current better than an insulator like glass, but not as well as such a conductor as copper.

sensor (SEHN suhr) a device that detects, monitors, or reports changes in the physical environment.

silicon (SIHL uh kuhn) a chemical element, it is a hard, dark-gray metalloid that has a shiny luster. Silicon is a semiconductor. A metalloid is a thing that is partly metal and partly nonmetal.

speed of light the fastest anything can travel, about 186,000 miles, (299,792 kilometers) per second. One of the first correct measurements of the speed of light was made in 1926 by scientist Albert Michelson.

star system a star or group of stars along with the planets and other objects that orbit it.

For further information

Want to learn more about stars?

Keranen, Rachel. *The Composition of the Universe: The Evolution of Stars and Galaxies.* Space Systems. Cavendish Square Publishing, 2017.

Want to learn more about the laws of motion?

Gianopoulos, Andrea. *Isaac Newton and the Laws of Motion.* Inventions and Discovery. Capstone Press, 2007.

Want to know more about the history of lasers?

Wyckoff, Edwin Brit. *The Man Who Invented the Laser: The Genuis of Theodore H. Mainman.* Genius Inventors and Their Great Ideas. Enslow Elementary, 2013.

Think like an inventor

Tiny electronic **probes** can explore places that otherwise are too small or far away for humans to reach. What are some places that tiny electronic probes could be used to explore?

Index

Acknowledgments

Cover	UCSB Experimental Cosmology Group
4-5	©Tunç Tezel
6-7	Ripton Scott (licensed under CC BY-SA 2.0)
8-9	ESO/M. Kornmesser; WORLD BOOK illustration by Matt Carrington
10-11	NASA
13	NASA
14-15	NASA/JHUAPL; NASA/JPL
16-17	UCSB Experimental Cosmology Group
18-19	© Shutterstock
21	U.S. Army
23	©Tim Boyle, Bloomberg/Getty Images; © Shutterstock
25	Philip Lubin
26-27	© Shutterstock
29	NASA
31	Philip Lubin
32-33	NASA/Goddard Space Flight Center/Tom Zagwodzki; WORLD BOOK diagram by Bensen Studios
34-35	UCSB Experimental Cosmology Group
37	Q. Zhang, NASA
38-39	ESO/M. Kornmesser
40-41	ESA/Hubble & NASA
43	Philip Lubin
44	Philip Lubin

www.ingramcontent.com/pod-product-compliance
Ingram Content Group UK Ltd.
Pitfield, Milton Keynes, MK11 3LW, UK
UKHW060103300726
14090UKWH00003B/369

* 9 7 8 0 7 1 6 6 6 1 3 5 1 *